This book is dedicated to all children.

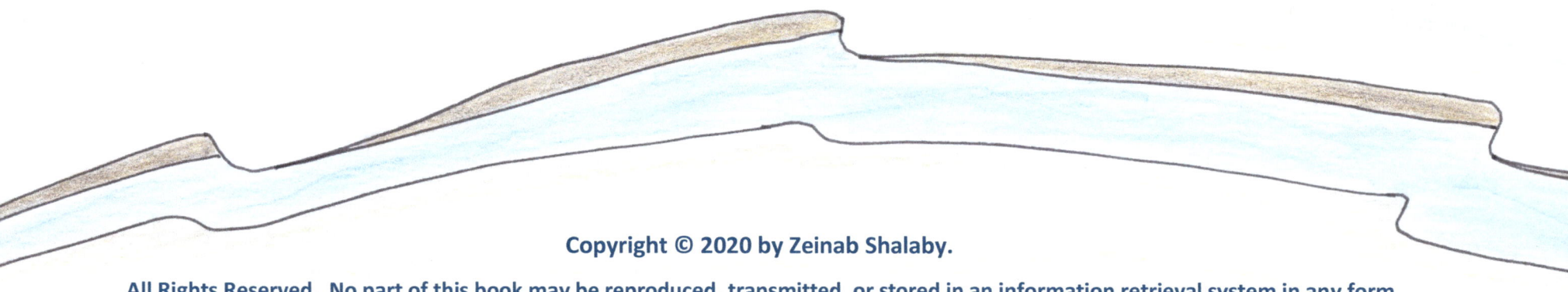

Copyright © 2020 by Zeinab Shalaby.

All Rights Reserved. No part of this book may be reproduced, transmitted, or stored in an information retrieval system in any form or by any means, graphic, electronic, or mechanical, including photocopying, taping, and recording, without prior written permission from the publisher.

First edition 2020

ISBN 978-1-959536-03-1

Edited by Noha Elmouelhi

Published by Honey Elm Books LLC

www.HoneyElmBooks.com

ABRAHAM:
The Friend of God

Written and illustrated by:

Zeinab Shalaby

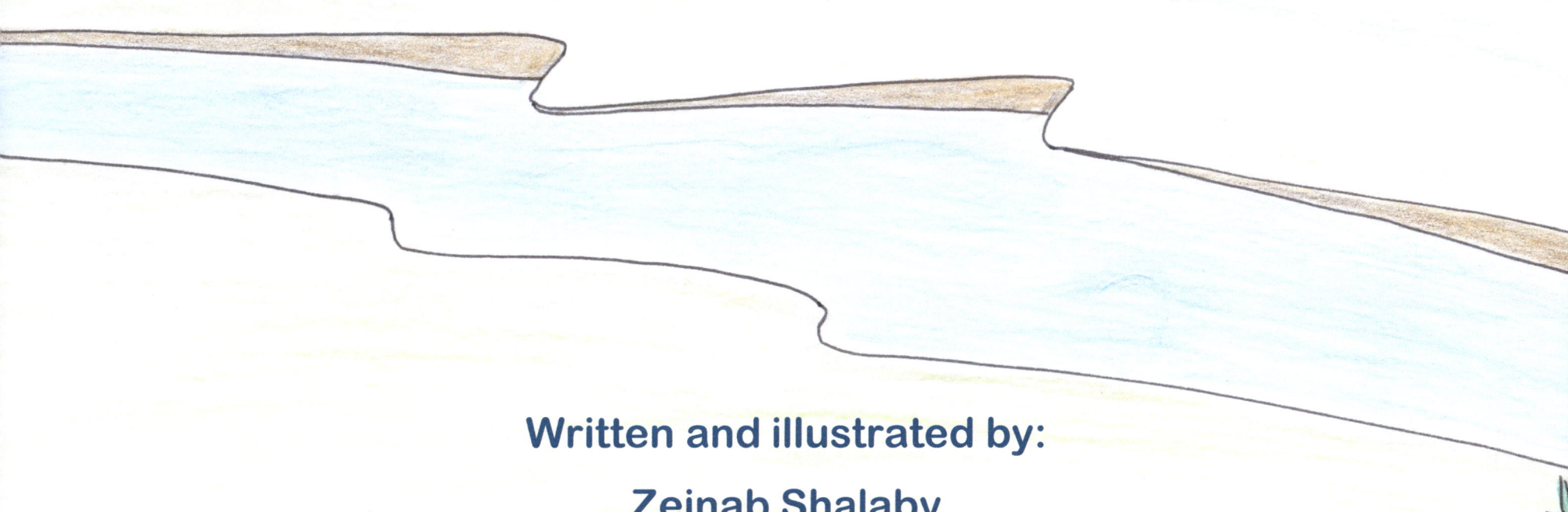

Abraham (PBUH) was born about 2000 years BC in what we know today as Iraq in Asia. The king of that country was very mean. Abraham's father, Aazar, was the chief of his clan. Do you know what people worshipped at that time?

PBUH = Peace Be Upon Him
BC = Before Christ
Clan = Group of People

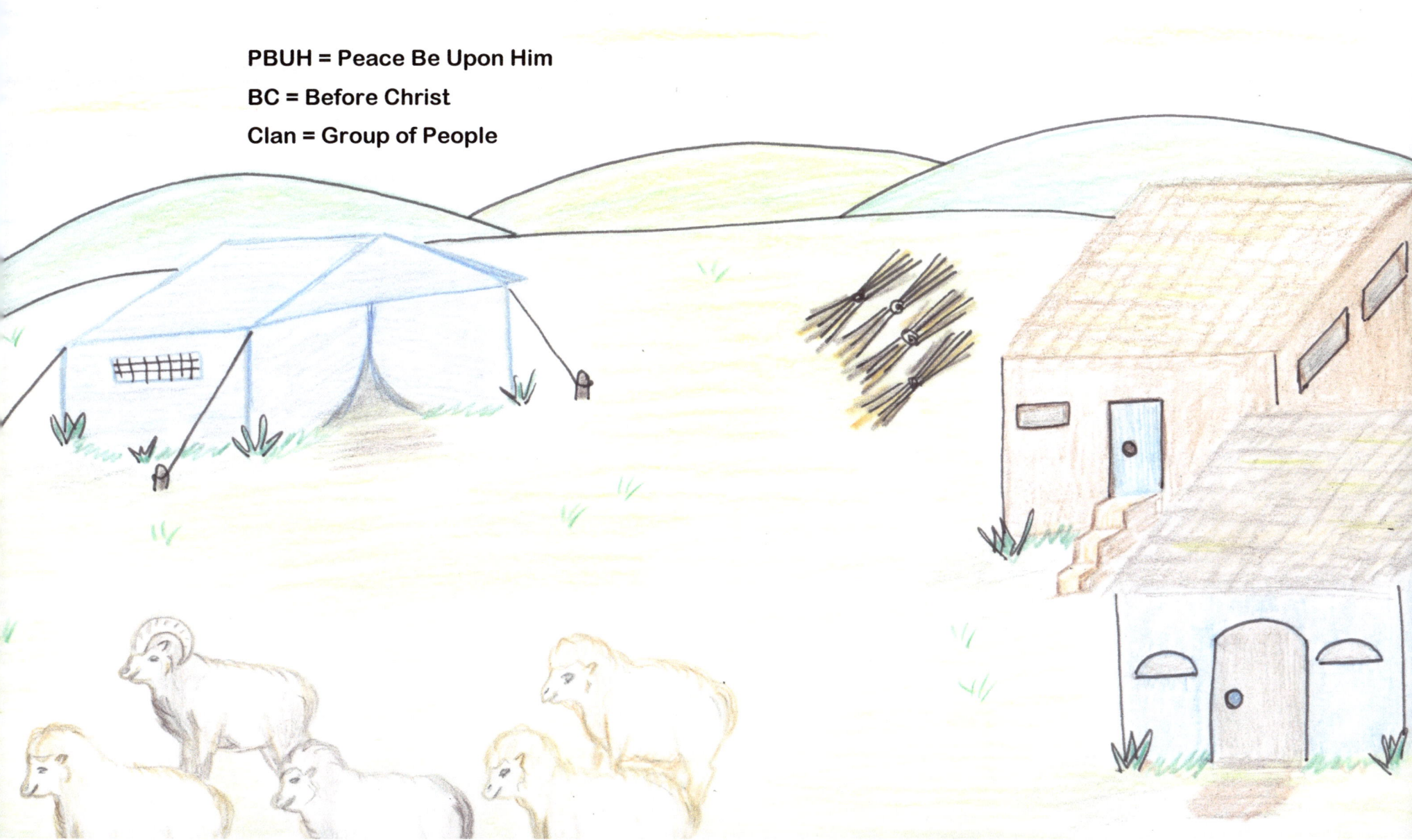

At that time, people worshipped idols and stars. Aazar used to make idols and sell them to his townspeople. Abraham did not believe in idol worshipping. But he did not know who created all the things around him, or whom he should worship.

Idols = Statues

As a young boy, Abraham started to look around him in search of God, wondering where He might be. One night, Abraham saw a star shining up in the sky. Abraham thought that the star might be God. Unfortunately, the next morning, it disappeared. What did Abraham think of that?

Abraham did not like it; he believed that God should not disappear. The next evening, while watching the sky, Abraham saw the moon. The moon was bigger and brighter than the star. Abraham said, "That might be God!" But the next morning, the moon disappeared too. Abraham was very disappointed.

The next day, Abraham saw the sun rising up in splendor. Immediately he said, "That is God, that is the biggest!" But the sun was not any better; that night it set and disappeared too. Did Abraham give up?

Splendor = Brilliance, Beauty

Abraham did not give up, but he was very confused. He believed that God must be mightier than all creatures. He thought that God should be in control of everything. He told his people that what they were doing was wrong, and he would never worship idols or stars. He prayed to his True God, and asked Him to guide him to the truth ... who is God?... and where is He?

God (the Exalted) answered Abraham's prayers. Abraham was told that there is only One God, and that God had created the whole universe: the heavens, the earth, and all creatures. Abraham now knew that humans should only worship God, and they should fear no one but God. Abraham now understood that God is everywhere. We cannot see God, but we can see His creations. God gave Abraham this special knowledge and asked him to help others to know the truth.

Abraham was very happy. He announced the truth to his father and all the townspeople. He asked them to worship the One and True God, and to abandon their idol-worshipping. But they refused to listen to him and asked him to stop bothering them. Did he stop? Did he leave the idols alone?

Abraham did not give up. At night, he went to the temple where they used to worship their idols, and destroyed all the idols with an axe, except the biggest one. Then, he hung the axe on the shoulder of the biggest idol and went home.

The next morning, the townspeople came to the temple to worship their idols as usual. They were very angry to see what had happened to their idols. Everyone thought it must have been Abraham who had done that. So, they went to the king and told him that Abraham had made fun of their idols by destroying all of the idols at the temple, except for the biggest one.

The king was furious. He ordered Abraham to be brought before him to be tried. They asked him, "Did you do that to our idols?" Abraham answered, "No, the biggest idol did it. Ask him…if he could speak!" Everyone was surprised and they said, "But idols can't talk!" So Abraham replied, "Then, why do you worship them?!? They cannot help you; they cannot hurt you. You should be ashamed of yourselves for worshipping anything other than God."

Abraham kept asking his townspeople to listen to the truth, and to believe in the One and True God. Still no one listened to him. The king ordered a big firepit to be built. Abraham was then thrown into the fire as punishment for insulting their gods and destroying them. But God protected Abraham from the fire. God ordered the fire to be cool, and not to harm Abraham. It was a miracle.

A few days later, the townspeople went to see what had happened to Abraham. To their surprise, Abraham was still alive, and the fire did not hurt him at all. They let him out of the firepit. Some people started to believe in the One and True God of Abraham. Among those who believed in God was his nephew, Lot, who became a prophet, too. Seeing that God had saved Abraham, the king left him alone.

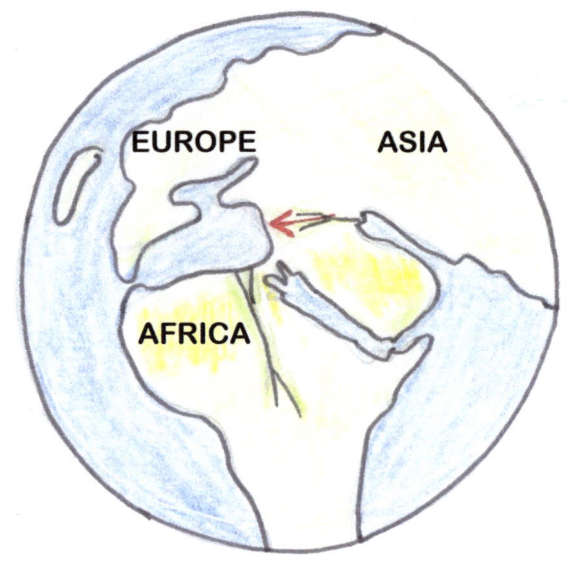

After the fire incident, some people began to listen to Abraham. He continued to preach to and advise his people for over fifty years. Still only a few believed in his message. Abraham decided to leave his country. He went west with his wife, Sarah, and his nephew, Lot. They settled in what we now call Palestine. In Palestine, both Abraham and Lot called on their people to believe in God and to obey Him.

Many years passed, and Abraham and Sarah were getting older. They never had children. Sarah suggested that Abraham should marry a younger woman named Hagar. Abraham married Hagar and he was very happy when she gave birth to a baby boy, Ishmael. After a while, Abraham took Hagar and Ishmael, according to God's will, to the south. When they reached the place we now call Mecca, Abraham left Hagar and baby Ishmael alone in the desert, with some food and water.

Before Abraham went back to Palestine, he prayed to God to help Hagar and Ishmael and to give them company. He knew that God would be with them.

For the first few days, Hagar nursed Ishmael. After a while, all the water and food were gone. Ishmael was very thirsty and he was crying all the time. Hagar was very sad; she tried to find water, but she failed. She ran between two mountains, which we now call Safa and Marwa, seven times in search of water. But there was none.

Suddenly, while Ishmael was kicking the sand, a lot of water sprang up. Hagar helped her son to drink and she drank too. Later on, many people came and lived next to them. From then on, they always had enough water, food, and company. This spring of water is still full of water today, and we call it Zamzam.

Ishmael grew up to be a smart, obedient boy. Abraham used to visit his wife, Hagar, and his son, Ishmael from time to time. One night, Abraham had a dream in which God commanded him to sacrifice his son. In the morning, Abraham told his son, Ishmael, about the dream, and asked him, "What do you think we should do?" Ishmael replied, "Oh father, do what you are ordered to do. I shall, by God's will, be patient." Did Abraham sacrifice his son? Did he obey God?

To sacrifice = To slay

Of course, Abraham obeyed God. As Abraham was about to sacrifice his beloved son, he heard a voice asking him to stop and to sacrifice a ram instead of his son. God had saved Ishmael. Do you know how we remember this every year? We celebrate Eid ul-Adha to remember this obedience of Abraham and Ishmael (PBUT) to God.

PBUT =

Peace Be Upon Them

Abraham proved his faith and that he loved no one more than God, and he obeyed nobody but God. God rewarded him and gave him another son from his very old wife, Sarah. They named their son, Isaac. He was very knowledgeable. Both Ishmael and Isaac would later become prophets.

A few years later, God asked Abraham to build a house next to Zamzam and to clean the place around it, so that the believers could worship God there. Very neatly, Abraham with the help of his son Ishmael built a house that looked like a cube. We call this house the Kaabah (the cube). We consider this place to be the holiest place on Earth. Can we visit this place now?

Abraham is a leader (imam) for all mankind. He had been so truthful and obedient to God that God called him "The Friend of God (Khalil Allah)". God rewarded him by choosing all of the next prophets from among his children and grandchildren. All prophets asked their people to believe in the One and True God and to follow His commands. As Muslims, we believe in the One and True God, and we believe in all the prophets too.

Now, let's imagine that Abraham PBUH is a big tree and see what the branches and leaves represent. They are the future generations of prophets that came from his progeny.

Progeny = children and grandchildren and their children and so on.

Did you know that the names in this story can be read in either English or Arabic?

English Name	Arabic Name	الإسم العربي
God	Allah	الله
Abraham	Ibrahim	إبراهيم
Lot	Lut	لوط
Ishmael	Ismail	إسماعيل
Isaac	Ishaq	إسحاق
Jacob	Yaqub	يعقوب
Joseph	Yusuf	يوسف
Moses	Musa	موسى
Jesus	Issa	عيسى
Mohamed	Muhammad	محمد
Sarah	Sarah	سارة
Hagar	Hagar	هاجر

www.ingramcontent.com/pod-product-compliance
Lightning Source LLC
Chambersburg PA
CBHW050848010526
44107CB00017BA/1217